PTSD: HORROR IN THE MIND

THE PSYCHOLOGY OF POST-TRAUMATIC STRESS DISORDER, AND THE ETHICAL WAY TO LIFT IT

MARK TYRRELL

uncommon knowledge™

First Publication 2015

ISBN 978-1-902892-31-3 ebook
ISBN 978-1-902892-37-5 paperback

Uncommon Knowledge Ltd
Boswell House,
Argyll Square
Oban
PA34 4BD

www.unk.com
support@unk.com

+44 (0) 1273 776770

CONTENTS

INTRODUCTION

Welcome to *PTSD: Horror in the Mind.*

Within these pages you'll learn how post-traumatic stress disorder (PTSD) presents, how it affects people, how to test for it, and how to test that it's gone. But most importantly, you'll learn to treat it – to help people overcome their own internal horror comfortably and quickly. And from personal experience, I can tell you that nothing is more rewarding.

I've treated thousands of traumatized people, from survivors of rape and attempted murder to people who've witnessed unspeakable death and destruction. I've successfully treated a kidnapping victim who believed he was about to be executed, a man who had his throat cut in a mugging, and traumatized soldiers from Iraq and Afghanistan.

But what I'm most proud of is that I've been able to train hundreds of other professionals to do the same. To ethically treat trauma *without* causing discomfort to the sufferer. Even as you read this, those professionals are out there, using the skills they've learned to improve fear-blighted lives quickly and permanently.

Before we get to the core articles, let me share with you a case that is particularly special to me. Some years ago, Matt came to me with extreme PTSD after serving in Afghanistan. His was a classic case of PTSD and clearly shows how the condition manifests.

Waves of horror just shopping in the mall

"A sickly sweet smell of melted flesh. The wave surges bringing the odor of vomit and bowels. Smack! It hits me again. A sea of red; human carnage on all sides. Screams for and from the dying. I don't even know I'm screaming until my throat dies on me, but still I scream silently.

"I'm all the way back in the heat of Helmand, but I'm not, because it might be a cold day in London.

"Say I'm out shopping for groceries or just walking in the park, and I hear the sound of a siren wailing from the street, or even the crash of a slammed door, or a car backfiring, or distant youths shouting, or the smell of smoke. And I'm right back there. It's not just a memory; it's like I'm actually there *again. I feel I'm about to die. There are no thoughts; just feelings. My war should have finished. It hasn't though. I can't live like this."*

Matt's horrifically evocative portrayal of the roadside bomb that he'd survived – while others hadn't – was so vivid I felt as though his words were not just telling but showing me something of the reality of the horror of that time and the way it now kept repeating on him, bleeding his life, torturing his nights.

But beneath the sympathy, I felt quietly pleased.

Why?

Because I knew I could make it go away. And I could do it right then and there. As a psychotherapist, there are few greater satisfactions than releasing someone from the torment of PTSD.

Because, for some, PTSD makes life itself a living nightmare – *until* it is effectively treated.

Haunted by horror

Flashbacks to past horrors eroding happiness and self-confidence. Nightmares ripping away restful sleep. And it's not just Matt. Every day, millions of people suffer with symptoms like these, and will continue to do so until they can be helped properly.

Rape, domestic and political torture, accident and illness, bullying and abuse. As if the experience and memory of the original horror weren't enough, PTSD sufferers find themselves dragged back to the same intense pain and fear every time they encounter the slightest subconscious trigger that in some small way, on some deep level, reminds them of that original trauma.

- A rustle in the grass from a playful kitten drives a woman to tears as she recalls being bitten and almost killed by a venomous grass snake over ten years ago.
- The sound of fireworks makes a man scream and tremble as it takes him back to the bomb attack he survived in a war decades earlier.
- A woman raped as a teenage girl by her uncle, a mechanic, suffers a full flashback at the mere whiff of petrol even as a middle-aged woman.

PTSD is not driven by thoughts – Matt hit the nail on the head when he said, "there are no thoughts; just feelings." Trying to treat PTSD at a *thinking* level rather than a *feeling* level is like trying to halt a forest fire by trying to reason with it.

Always remember, fundamentally, it is *emotion* we are dealing with.

But what, fundamentally, are emotions for? I think it's useful, just quickly, to consider this.

Feelings keep you alive

Emotions are for survival. We feel scared, angry, worried or guilty when something threatens, or *seems* to threaten, our wellbeing in some way.

Emotions are signals. When a need *isn't* met, they signal this to us through feelings such as anxiety, guilt, anger, or misery. These signals encourage us to seek out this need. At the most basic level, they are there to keep us alive! But they also let us know when a need *is* met – through feelings such as satisfaction, happiness, and contentment.

In primitive environments, this emotional signaling system is really efficient. But with the complex challenges posed by the modern world, it can become confused, sometimes to the point where it can cause all kinds of emotional problems.

So *why* do people become traumatized? *Why* did nature endow us with the characteristic of being able to be so badly traumatized?

Of what possible evolutionary use is it?

Better safe than sorry

When someone has PTSD, it means their brain has *learned* something. And learned something very well.

Humans' capacity for this deep and sudden learning evolved for the same reason as most other characteristics – because it enhanced our survival. Cast your mind back a few thousand years and imagine a tribal man wandering across a barren plain into a crop of trees.

Suddenly, he becomes aware of the movement of grass at the base of a tree. He barely has time to register the motion before a snarling lion pounces upon him.

Paralyzed with fear, he knows there is no escape. Death feels certain. Then, just in the nick of time, his tribe appears to rescue him. Physically, the damage is minimal – he survives with a few shallow lacerations and grazes. But mentally, the learning experience was deep.

A month later, his wound have healed completely. He is walking through some trees with his fellow tribe members, far from where the incident occurred. Just then a gust of wind rustles through the grass at the base of a tree and, much to the surprise of his unsuspecting tribe, he screams and runs, shaking and sweating.

He reacted *as if* those different trees were the same trees as before, *as if* the movement in the grass was again caused by a lion, *as if* he was again going to be mauled.

You see, to maximize our chances of survival the mind needs to *err on the side of caution*. Your brain *needs* to make sloppy matches in that way in order to keep you alive.

The part of the brain in control of this process is the amygdala, which is deeply involved with memory processing, emotions, and decision-making – but not logic! This means that anything that even *vaguely* reminds the brain of the original trauma sets off the flight or fight reaction again.

So what's the problem?

When survival solutions become problems in themselves

Our brain's 'sloppy pattern matching,' erring on the side of caution, is *essential* in natural environmental situations where lives are at stake. In nature, the potential cost of *not* reacting is so high that *overreacting* helps us survive.

If you respond to a vine as if it's a snake, that's clearly better than *not* responding to a snake when it really is one.

But in a fast-paced modern world, the situation is a little more complex. The downside of making faulty matches in a totally natural setting is minimal, whereas the downside of reacting to every car as if it contains a suicide bomber is massive. Especially if your life *requires* you to be around cars.

The complexities of modern life can turn potentially life-saving 'sloppy' emotional responses into major problems.

PTSD is incredibly powerful, but it's not complicated. Likewise, successfully treating PTSD is just as powerful and, if you're equipped with the right knowledge and tools, can be just as uncomplicated.

But there is an art as well as a science to it.

Unhooking the horror: How treatments vary

Treatments for trauma are almost always planned and undertaken with the very best of intentions. But the reality is that many of them are at best unreliable and uncomfortable, and at worst cruel and painful.

PTSD has often been treated by having sufferers confront their nightmarish memories head on. But for the one in four people who seem to be naturally prone to long-term PTSD, trying to talk about the trauma can actually reinforce the memory and the emotions that come along with it. In other words, a treatment that aims to *reduce* the effect of painful memories can actually *increase* their power.

So how do we help trauma sufferers effectively and ethically? What do mental health professionals need to know?

The three essential principles of ethical trauma relief

Treatment for PTSD should be:

1. Fast. A person can become traumatized in a fraction of a second. And just like that, the brain has learned an emotional response pattern. It makes sense, then, that the treatment should be quick as well. A one-off traumatic memory can usually be resolved comfortably within 20 to 30 minutes. If someone is in pain, we need to help them as quickly as possible – and with the right treatment, we can.

2. Dissociated. The brain needs to process a traumatic memory as a *narrative*. This is why traumatic events are turned into stories and even legends in some cultures. For example, traumatized children in war-torn African countries sometimes repeatedly re-enact a trauma, perhaps with toy weapons, as a way of trying to process it.[1] Often when they are encouraged to alter 'the story' in some way, they will feel a greater sense of control over the event, and will experience less anxiety.

When we are able to put trauma outside of ourselves, it can reside as a historical memory in the cerebral cortex of the brain. But until we dissociate from the memory in this way, it nests agonizingly in the 'flight or fight' part of the brain, the amygdala, to be relived every time the memory is triggered.

Dissociation is a natural part of how the brain processes trauma and, in fact, any painful memory. Using dissociation in treatment means the memory can be viewed more objectively and finally put to bed. When this happens, the memory no longer fires off uncontrollably, but becomes something the person can choose to think about calmly if they wish.

Dissociation can be likened to anesthesia for the mind, allowing you to get to work 'surgically' moving the memory from where it hurts to where it can live comfortably, healthily, and safely. But without the 'anesthesia' of dissociation you may never even be able to get near the memory.

3. Deeply calm. Trauma treatment needs to be comfortable. Once a traumatic memory is accessed quickly from a comfortable, dissociated, and, crucially, *profoundly* relaxed state, then the memory can be retagged as no longer threatening *incredibly quickly* (even if the trauma stems from decades before).

The memory is retagged as past, not present. Memories bound up with the amygdala don't fade like other memories, and always feel current or recent until they are freed from the influence of the 'flight or fight' amygdala.

So what is it like when people are quickly freed from trauma?

Free at last

Typically after a traumatic memory has been ethically healed you'll hear people say things like:

- "It no longer feels important."
- "It feels really distant now, and I can think about it with total calm."
- "I know it was terrible at the time, but it no longer *feels* terrible to think about it. It's like something from the long ago past that no longer matters. It's really distant!"

ONE
POPULAR TREATMENT MODELS FOR PTSD

Some popular treatment methods use one or more of the three ethical principles to treat trauma.

Critical incident debriefing

Critical incident debriefing (CID) involves encouraging the victim of a recent trauma to discuss what happened and describe their feelings.

How many of the three ethical principles does CID incorporate?

CID doesn't really use any of the principles. That's why CID can be a toxic treatment for people most at risk of developing long-term PTSD: not just ineffective, but painful and counterproductive.

Eye movement desensitization and reprocessing

Eye movement desensitization and reprocessing (EMDR) involves encouraging the trauma survivor to think and/or talk about the traumatic incident while experiencing rapid eye movement (REM). A therapist may ask the client to focus on their pen or a light as it moves from side to side. This does seem to help some – though not all – people reprocess traumatic memories away from the amygdala's influence so the memory can be experienced as narrative: past and non-threatening.

How many of the three ethical principles does EMDR incorporate?

EMDR uses more of the three ethical principles than CID. It uses dissociation and, if it works, can be quick. But because it doesn't major on relaxation, for some it can be ineffective and still quite painful.

The emotional freedom technique

The emotional freedom technique (EFT), sometimes known as 'tapping therapy', is a method in which a person accesses their distressing memories or thoughts while various parts of their body are exposed to repeated physical pressure ('tapping'). The trauma sufferer can perform the treatment themselves, or a therapist can administer it. EFT can aid with weight loss, unpleasant and limiting thoughts, trauma, and phobias among other applications.

How many of the three ethical principles does EFT incorporate?

Again, EFT can be quick if it works for someone. And it uses the second aspect of ethical trauma treatment, dissociation. Constant tapping on the skin while reviewing a traumatic memory can help distract focus in the brain, indicating to the amygdala that this memory must no longer be so significant because focus is now fractured (partly on the memory and partly on the tapping).

It's not the tapping itself that helps, it's the fact that it distracts you. If you asked someone to recall a traumatic event while simultaneously reciting the alphabet, that too may go some way towards retagging the memory as less traumatic.

But relaxation doesn't feature in EFT, and while the tapping does provide some degree of dissociation, it is hindered by the lack of deep calm, making this method somewhat unreliable.

Some proponents of EFT promote the idea that it accesses invisible meridian energy channels, perhaps not understanding the three ethical trauma treatment principles or, specifically, the role of distraction/dissociation in the technique, and how this works to detraumatize the brain.

So is there a technique that uses all three ethical principles?

The Rewind Technique

The Rewind Technique is a relatively new way of working on specific traumatic and/or phobic memories. It can also be used to reduce fear and anxiety associated with future events, perhaps even *preventing* trauma.

The technique applies profound relaxation to disengage the traumatic memory from the 'flight or fight' center of the brain. It engages the imagination to allow the trauma survivor to review the memory from a safe, secure, double-dissociated vantage point. The person is then encouraged to experience the memory in 'rewind' (backwards), which quickly strips the kinesthetic effect (including fear) from the memory. Only then do they get to watch the memory from a single dissociated point of view while deeply calm and relaxed. Just for good measure, the process is repeated three times for each memory. Encouraging the person to view their likely future now the trauma or phobia has gone further deepens the positive impact.

How many of the three ethical principles does the Rewind Technique incorporate?

The Rewind Technique uses all three of the ethical principles. It's deeply relaxing and therefore protective and safe. It uses not just dissociation but *double* dissociation. And it's fast. Not only that, it can be used to rehearse future reactions as well as change current ones.

It can be used for *any* type of trauma, mild or severe, past or future. And its inherently non-voyeuristic nature makes it perfect to use with clients who are uncomfortable or ashamed to relate the nature of their traumas.

Any technique that utilizes all three principles of ethical trauma treatment is likely to be effective – but you may be hard pressed to find a method that encapsulates and concentrates them as efficiently as Rewind.

I used Rewind with Matt. This poor man, physically and mentally drained from the ongoing effects of his trauma, was finally relaxed. He couldn't believe the power of Rewind! I could hear the change in his voice when he told me, "I can think about it but it's like... way over there now. I feel properly free to be sad for my comrades who died on that day, but I don't feel scared at all when I recall it." The memory became something that *felt* past. The nightmares and flashbacks stopped, and everyday life events no longer triggered feelings of horror or anxiety – or even mild discomfort. Matt never took any of the medication his doctor had prescribed him. He didn't need to.

Good practitioners practice evidence-based medicine, and I know some of you will be reading this asking, "Where's the evidence?" It's a fair question. Until recently, treatment of trauma has been quite primitive, often based on poor science and minimal evidence. But with the Rewind Technique, the principles are there, and early research by the Human Givens Institute is extremely promising.[1] In an initial study of 30 people, 93% of clients rated the Rewind Technique as either successful or extremely successful, with the remaining 7% saying it was acceptable. Clients reported massive improvements in quality of life, rating their wellbeing at an average of 12 out of 50 before treatment and 30.3 at 7–10 days post-treatment. This increased by another 2 points over the following 3–6 months.

Before this study twenty six of the forty seven participants met the criteria for Post Traumatic Stress Disorder (PTSD). After the trial none of the forty seven met the PTSD criteria. Murphy, the study author, suggests the treatment is suitable for all ages from as low as eight years old to patients much older in their seventies and said: "The case notes repeatedly identified not only relief from symptoms but also the emergence of qualitative positive changes in the individuals' daily lives."

I would ask you to evaluate the Rewind Technique based on the principles behind it, and at the very least to remain *open* to it. Existing research may be somewhat limited in scope, but the results are still pretty amazing. This is just the beginning for Rewind, and I know the next few decades will see plenty of strong evidence coming forth.

In these pages we'll review real cases of horrendous trauma and you'll see how the Rewind Technique has been able to help people quickly, effectively, and without further trauma. You'll get a full sense of just how PTSD presents, how to spot it, and how it can be lifted once and for all.

Successfully treating trauma is one of the most meaningful things you can ever do.

This book is for you

This book is a collection of articles I've written on trauma over years of working in the field. You'll hear stories of desperately brave survivors from all kinds of traumas.

I hope you enjoy the different angles and ideas and solutions presented in this book.

All the best,

Mark Tyrrell

TWO

IS YOUR CLIENT TRAUMATIZED?

HOW TO TELL IF A MEMORY NEEDS TO BE DECONDITIONED

"My mother put her hands tight around my throat and squeezed. I started to pass out. This happened right outside our front door. I one hundred per cent believed I was going to die. The look on her face was... business-like... there was no way she was going to stop – until I was dead."

Ellie related this horrific story to me quite calmly. Fortunately, a neighbor had seen what was happening and intervened. Ellie's mother eventually "went away for a while" – she had been institutionalized.

You may be surprised to learn that Ellie was not left traumatized by this experience.

She had actually come to see me for help with weight loss. She shared the story of her mother's life-threatening actions with me only as part of the general background information about her childhood.

I took steps to check that Ellie really didn't need help reprocessing her memory of such a disturbing experience, and then we got down to work on her motivation to exercise and eat well.

So how did I know that we didn't need to focus on her mother's attempt to murder her?

The incredible shrinking memory

Contrary to popular belief, not everyone who has been through a horrendous experience is traumatized by it. Around 75% of survivors of trauma naturally recover from a traumatic event without any kind of intervention.[1] Most people process traumatic experience by dreaming it out, or talking it out, or otherwise contextualizing it – just as Ellie had done years ago.

The 25% of trauma survivors who have persistent post-traumatic stress symptoms – such as flashbacks, nightmares, and generalized anxiety disorder – are vulnerable for various reasons, but three factors seem to be commonly implicated.

People who fall into this category typically

- were suffering from anxiety before the trauma occurred
- were exposed to a greater degree of trauma, and
- are naturally more hypnotizable.

Now why should that be?

Trance – a double-edged sword

It's interesting that people who are better hypnotic subjects are more prone to developing long-term PTSD.[2]

However, it *makes sense* that the more hypnotizable

someone is, the more prone they are to developing PTSD or phobias in appropriate circumstances. Fortunately, that correlation also means that they are easy to treat.

What is quickly caused (a trauma can be 'learnt' in a matter of seconds) can also be quickly lifted – if not in seconds, at least in minutes.

But if most people naturally contextualize what happened to them and don't need help, how do we, as therapists, know who needs help deconditioning a traumatic memory and who doesn't?

You can make this determination using three simple questions.

1) Can they actually talk about it?

In so-called 'critical incident debriefing', the traumatized person is asked to talk about what happened to them as soon after the event as possible. This approach has now been shown to be counterproductive for many survivors of trauma.[3,4]

This might be okay for the 70% or so of people who would have recovered naturally anyway. But for people in the more vulnerable group – who are likely to be more severely traumatized – talking about it, or trying to relate what happened in words, can actually worsen the trauma in the brain by 'reactivating' it and embedding it deeper.

If your client can't talk about a trauma, don't push it. Until you have detraumatized the memory, talking about it will only make it worse.

2) Does it still feel recent?

Many therapists assume that someone *must* be holding on to trauma if they have been through something awful.

But why?

The brain is magnificently adaptive. Some people *don't* need help overcoming a trauma. They fall within the 75% of people who are able to talk it out, as Ellie had (although, of course, the more severe the traumatic experience the more likely it is that help will be required).

I asked Ellie to tell me whether, when she thought about the time her mother had tried to kill her, she felt anxious right now, forty years later.

"It was terrifying at the time!"

"Yes, but does it make you feel scared now, just recalling it?"

"No, because I know it's way in the past. It feels like a long time ago."

This told me that this memory, terrible though it was, was no longer 'live' for Ellie.

Because of the way trauma gets 'lodged' in the brain, traumatic memories don't tend to fade with time until they are 'detraumatized'. (I use the Rewind Technique to do this as it is the safest and fastest method I know of).

Another client of mine, who was in her sixties, recalled finding herself hanging by her fingers from a loft opening when her brother, for a laugh, pulled the ladder out from beneath her feet. She told me that this 50-year-old memory still felt like it happened only yesterday.

Ask your client whether the traumatic incident feels more recent than it actually was when it comes to mind.

3) Do even nebulous 'reminders' set off flashbacks?

A war veteran I saw would feel terrified at the sound of fireworks or other sudden noises. He also felt compelled to walk down the middle of the road (in spite of the obvious dangers!) because back in Afghanistan roadside bombs had been common and deadly.

A woman who had been raped by a man with a beard would have flashbacks at the sight of a bearded man. That's a lot of flashbacks.

You can, of course, ask someone straight out whether they still get flashbacks to the event, but to show them that you really understand how trauma works you can ask them whether even the vaguest of reminders sets off a huge panic response within them.

Deep within the brain of someone with PTSD, the amygdala has been 'imprinted' with the pattern of the trauma they've experienced. This imprint consists of all the information surrounding the initial event – including aspects not available to conscious memory.[5] Once this traumatic template is in place, the amygdala compares all incoming information to that template. The moment it detects a match – however tenuous – it fires into action, without conscious reason or logic.

This is your key. If even minor elements of the pattern of the initial incident set off panic, then your client is in need of detraumatization.

Ellie came to me to lose weight – and lose weight she did. But she was right not to seek help for her trauma – she had put it behind her decades before. To have treated her for trauma would have been a waste of both of our time.

THREE
COULD IT BE PTSD?
THREE KEY QUESTIONS THAT WILL HELP YOU FIND OUT

She kept fainting, and it was ruining her young life.

She'd had it all: PET, EEG, CT, fMRI... and that was only the tests I'd actually heard of! They'd found nothing.

Emily's mother Jane brought her to me for hypnosis, but Emily, intelligent and articulate at 15, did most of the talking.

"I hate this! My friends go on about how they'd like to change their body shape, or something about their face, but the only thing I want to change is this, to stop fainting!"

Emily told me how she had fainted while out boating on a school trip to France and had to be rescued. School trips were now out for her. She told me how she'd fainted on the stairs at school, and fallen half way down the flight, obliviously unconscious. She rolled up her sleeve and showed me the lingering scar on her forearm. So now she was no longer allowed upstairs at school.

She explained how she couldn't accept invitations for sleepovers, because she was worried about passing out at a friend's house (although it had only ever happened at school).

I didn't like what I was thinking, but I had to wonder...

Is there a payoff?

Uncharitably, albeit briefly, I wondered whether Emily was getting some kind of subconscious pay off for her proneness to falling unconscious. Certainly she'd been marked out for special treatment, and had received an unusual amount of attention and compassion.

But this explanation just didn't *feel* quite right to me.

Emily told me she'd had months of therapy with a cognitive behavioral therapist, analyzing her every thought. But if anything, this only made her feel *more* anxious. In fact, she believed her fainting episodes had actually become more frequent as a result.

Could there have been some traumatic basis to all this? I used three questions to find out.

Three questions that help in diagnosing PTSD

Question 1: Did anything in particular happen around the time the symptom first occurred?

This seems so obvious, yet it's surprising how often it gets missed. (I'm ashamed to admit that it was not until my second session with Emily that I got around to this question myself!)

I asked Emily how long she had lived with these life restricting fainting fits.

"About two years now."

"And did anything happen to upset you around the time they started?"

Here Emily's mum Jane interjected: "Well, actually, there were a couple of upsetting things back then, weren't there Emily...?"

It turned out that Emily had been very close to their 70-year-old neighbor, Pam. Seemingly much younger than her years, Pam was a vibrant and lively woman who was like a grandmother to Emily. When Emily came home from school one day to hear that she had suddenly died, it was a terrible shock.

But there was more to come.

Only a few weeks later, Emily returned from school to yet another awful shock. The beloved family dog had been run over in the street and killed.

"Come to think of it," said Jane, "it *was* just around that time that you started fainting at school, Emily..."

It's incredible how metaphorical the human mind can be.

These two deaths had occurred when Emily was not at home. She was at school. Her brain had tagged 'school' as, if not the cause of, then at least associated with, the death of loved ones.

Of course she knew consciously that the deaths of her beloved neighbor and her darling dog were completely unconnected to herself and her actions or whereabouts. But her subconscious mind had made a link.

When we are traumatized, our brain tries to complete patterns through dreaming, talking, rituals, or metaphors. In Emily's case, fainting at school became a metaphor for 'dying'.

This was a neat explanation but, determined not to assume anything, I pushed my theories aside. I explored further.

Question 2: Does it make you really upset to talk about it, even now?

This is such an important part of assessing whether a particular memory needs detraumatizing.

"Emily, when you think about that time when your dad

told you about Pam, does it still feel raw and painful, even now, two years later?"

Emily took a few seconds to recall the moment she'd heard of Pam's unexpected death. Tears appeared in her eyes and she began to shake a little.

That was all I needed.

It was the same with the dog. Emily said even thinking about hearing the news made her feel "just as upset as I did at the time".

It sounds obvious, but the quickest way to find out whether you need to treat trauma is simply to ask "Does it hurt now when you think about it?"

Which leads into the third way of assessing trauma.

Question 3: Has time stood still?

Traumatic memories become trapped between the amygdala (where the 'fight or flight' response originates) and the hippocampus (where recent memories are stored). Instead of fading with time like normal memories, they remain as vivid and painful as the day they were formed.

Neutral or pleasant memories are transferred to the neocortex (where long-term memories are stored), and start to feel distant with time. But when traumatic memories don't get transferred into long-term memory, they become persistent – unless we help get them there.

I have worked with many traumatized people, some with traumas stretching back to the 1940s. But their memories of these traumas, no matter how long ago they were, all felt recent, or even current.

Emily told me that when she thought about the two times she had come home from school to terrible news, it didn't feel like two years had passed at all. It felt like it "happened yesterday." In fact, Emily told us, "I can still see Dad standing by the kitchen door, telling me Pam is dead. I can see his face, it feels like it's happening right now."

I asked Emily if she'd like to "put those memories where they belong, in the past" and she said she would. I also suggested to Emily and her mother Jane that I couldn't be sure, but I thought the fainting may very well stop once those memories had been detraumatized.

Emily's new hope

I helped Emily by using the Rewind Technique to decondition the painful emotion from those memories so they no longer had power over her.

She could always feel a little sad whenever she chose to think about Pam or her dog. After the Rewind, we tested how Emily felt about those memories now and she told me something I often hear after a Rewind session: "It feels all faded and really distant now... like it was a very long time ago..."

So the takeaway for uncovering trauma is:

- Don't assume there *must* be a traumatic root to a troublesome symptom but be aware there *might* be. Ask if anything upsetting occurred before or around the time the symptom first started.
- Ask if it *still* hurts even now (*not* if it hurt at the time) and if they say yes, ask them to think about that time.
- Ask if the memory feels more recent than it should, considering how long ago the event occurred.

Emily's sad memories were put in the past where they belonged. And she never fainted at school again.

FOUR

IS IT CRUCIAL TO IDENTIFY THE INITIAL EVENT THAT CREATED A TRAUMA PATTERN?

WHY FINDING THE ROOT CAUSE OF A TRAUMA WILL NOT LIFT IT

As part of the online course I run teaching therapists the Rewind Technique, I offer interactive Q&A teaching sessions. I've received great feedback from these sessions, where students can fill any gaps in their understanding of how the technique works and ask questions to make sure they are fully prepared to implement the technique in their own practice. It's one of the most rewarding parts of my job.

Now and then I get the chance to answer a question that really gets to the heart of how the Rewind Technique works. This is one of those questions.

"I have a new client who experienced physical and emotional abuse as a child, in the Imprint period, around 6–7 years of age. After a couple of sessions it's become clear that there may be a couple of significant events, during the Imprint period, that may have anchored a pattern of learned helplessness, and in turn developed into anxiety and depression as an adult for

this person. Is it crucial to identify the very first event which created the trauma pattern, or will applying the technique on similar though later episodes delete the entire problem/gestalt?"

To answer this question in a couple of sentences:

- It's not always essential to discover the initial cause of a trauma.
- If the memory is not troubling, there's no need to delve into it. It's the 'active' memories that need our attention.

But let's take a more in-depth look at *why*.

Therapists have been known to get a little too hung up on discovering the root cause of a trauma – that initial experience that instigated the problem, and may still be maintaining the problem in the here and now. Perhaps this is partly a remnant of the Freudian principles of psychology. But the truth is, we don't always necessarily *need* to get back to that initial memory.

If a client doesn't *know* why they are phobic or traumatized, if they don't *recall* the original memory, there's a good chance it's no longer actively maintaining their traumatized state. It might have been forgotten precisely *because* it is no longer an active trauma-maintaining memory in and of itself. That can happen. Sometimes you'll talk to someone with a phobia and they'll talk about the memory they believe stimulated the phobia with complete calm.

They'll say, "When I was five and this happened..."

If I can see that the memory doesn't seem to be bothering them, that's when I'll cut in. "When you think about that time, do you feel anxious?"

And they'll say "No, I don't actually, but I remember a time last year, when I was 30, that I saw a spider and it made me feel really anxious."

That tells me that their mind has already processed the initial experience and we don't need to work on that. We need to work on what is actually *active* in this person's brain as far as the trauma or phobia is concerned. We need to focus on the times they can actually *remember* feeling really scared.

In the course itself I use the example of an adult who may have developed a phobia of buttons at a very young age when memories were laid down and recalled differently.

You see, in the early years we have what are called snapshot memories, they are only called narrative memories as the brain develops.

Say a six-month-old puts a button in their mouth, and an adult, not wanting them to swallow the button, panics, shouting out and startling the baby.

In this moment, the child may develop a conditioned fear response to buttons – but never know why.

He will probably never recall the memory of being six months old, but as he grows he will continually respond to buttons with fear and alarm. These intense responses will create strong and lasting memories.

They may recall specific experiences with buttons at age 6, or 16, or 33. They may recall these experiences as if they were recent, as if those emotions are still active. That's how you know these are the memories you need to work on.

And by working on those recalled memories, we effectively undo the work of that initial experience. We don't have to work on that initial experience. We may not even be *able* to work on it, as it may be beyond the reaches of memory. But we can change the pattern without having to know the very first experience – which may not even be fueling adult anxiety anymore.

FIVE

WHY THERE'S NO NEED TO RELIVE THE TRAUMA ALL OVER AGAIN

WHICH PTSD TREATMENTS CAN MAKE THINGS WORSE, AND WHY

"My father murdered my mother. Right in front of me and my brother. The police came and took my dad away, and eventually he was put in a secure psychiatric hospital. After that, me and John went to live with our grandparents. That's when the real trouble started."

June related these awful memories from her remote past with no noticeable sign of being upset by them. Her voice was calm. She was just telling me the facts.

"Do you get flashbacks to the murder?" I asked her. "Do you get nightmares that seem to relate to that time?"

"No," she said. "I know it seems weird, but I really feel like I came to terms with all that a long time ago."

June was 48 years old when we met. She had never talked about her past, and had never had any therapy, except for some "psychoanalytical stuff" that had been "worse than useless."

"What did you mean, June, when you said that the real

trouble started when you went to live with your grandparents?" I asked her.

"They used to beat us," she said. "They beat me and John for anything really. I think they enjoyed it. But that wasn't the worst of it."

When talking makes things worse

I was studying June's face as she was talking. And I saw it. The burning flicker of pure fear – fleeting, but unmistakable. It pervaded her eyes, her mouth, each and every muscle of her face. It was as if an invisible sharp wind had whipped across a still, glassy lake.

"When I was twelve my uncle also came to live with us. *That's* when..."

She paused, seeming to be struggling to find words. I didn't push. In fact, I felt it was important she *didn't* tell me too much. But gradually she revealed her story.

Her uncle was a car mechanic and worked in a field at the back of the house. He would wake her up at night, drag her down to his makeshift mechanic garage, and brutally rape her. Hundreds of times she was ravaged and humiliated, before finally fleeing her twisted travesty of a family at eighteen, never to return.

June's uncle had never been arrested. June told me she didn't care what had happened to him; she just wanted to feel safe again. Now, thirty years later, she was working two jobs, in a relationship she didn't feel was right for her, running for two hours a day to "get rid of the anxiety," and waking up every few hours through the night sweating and screaming. Worst of all, the mere smell of engine oil would bring on a terrifying flashback of being raped.

"I don't drive or go anywhere near cars if I can avoid it."

June needed help, clearly. I knew how to help her. And I fully intended to help her.

But suppose June had not come to see me. Suppose she had gone elsewhere. What kind of 'help' could she have expected to get...?

Back into hell

It has long been recognized that people who have been through very traumatic experiences often need help to recover fully. A long-established approach is to get victims to 'relive' their trauma, either by 'talking it through' or even, most cruelly, by hypnotically reliving it as if it were happening in the here and now.

And what's wrong with this? Everything.

Talking about the trauma, even just trying to put what happened into words, can actually worsen a victim's trauma by re-activating it in the brain, and embedding it deeper.

Dr. Noreen Tehrani, an occupational health and counselling psychologist specializing in post-traumatic stress, explains what happens: "If a trauma victim is debriefed in a state of high emotion, the process can increase the arousal to the point of overload, trapping the sensory impressions in the amygdala."

This is why so called 'critical incident debriefing', where disaster survivors are encouraged to 'talk it out', can be a disaster for the 25% of people who remain severely traumatized after an event.[1]

Getting people to 'relive' their trauma is *not* therapy.

Think about it. If 'reliving' a trauma could heal PTSD, the first real flashback would do the trick.[2]

You might remember from the last article that 75% of people affected by trauma will not go on to develop persistent PTSD. For them, talking it out may be merely unhelpful. But for the remaining 25% it can be downright dangerous.[3]

So how *can* the one in four people who are likely to develop long lasting PTSD get over their trauma?

Exorcising haunted minds

"Even the smells come flooding back... it just needs the smallest reminder..."

June's experiences of reliving the nightmarish assaults from her uncle in flashback are typical of people suffering long-term effects of trauma.

June could talk about all kinds of other horrors quite calmly. But as soon as she tried to talk about the rapes she became acutely upset and struggled to speak. The memories were lodged in a part of the brain beyond language.

I told her that there was no need for her to give me details. It was bad enough that she'd had to live through these experiences the first time around.

I used the Rewind Technique to help her *without* needing to know the details of her experiences.

But what is 'trauma' anyway?

How your memories are made

Normally, memories are laid down as immediate impressions in the brain, organized to become coherent in the hippocampus, and finally stored in the neocortex as 'long-term memories'. This process turns a remembered event into a 'narrative memory' – something you can talk about, that feels past, and that eventually fades with time.

However, when people are traumatized, this process can be

blocked. The traumatic memory may never get turned into narrative.

Imagine all your worst memories feeling 'live' –as if they are happening now – even if they happened half a lifetime ago.

PTSD – the memories that won't fade

This is the reality for PTSD sufferers – the memory doesn't fade with time. It feels absolutely current and impossible to talk about. I once worked with a man who had been traumatized in World War II. Nearly 60 years later, he told me his horrendous experiences felt like they happened only a week ago!

During a traumatic event a person's emotional response can be so extreme that the memory becomes encoded in the 'fight or flight' part of the brain, the amygdala, instead of the hippocampus. It stays 'locked' in this part of the brain as a survival pattern, ready to reactivate if a similar emergency should arise again.

As we discussed in the introduction, this is a useful process – in theory. But in reality, this sloppy process can mean that a fear pattern is reactivated by quite incidental elements from the original trauma.

We've already looked at a couple of examples. Remember Matt, who felt like he was about to die every time a car backfired? Or June, who would relapse into memories of childhood rape every time she smelt engine oil? These weren't logical responses – they were deeply encoded emotional responses.

As I said, most people who go through a trauma will eventually reprocess the memory though the hippocampus, to eventually be stored in the neocortex as a past event. They know it was horrendous *at the time*, but it no longer makes them feel terrified to recall it. The memory fades.

But for PTSD sufferers, recalling the memory is as horrendous as the experience itself – they feel they are right 'back there', in that awful time. Talking about it, for these people, will make things worse, because the pattern just gets reactivated.

So what *does* help?

Healing haunted minds

An effective trauma relief treatment must be able to generate both sufficient *dissociation* and sufficient *calm* in the sufferer to allow the painful memory to be reprocessed safely, so that it can be moved, so to speak, from the '*now*-focused' fight or flight amygdala to the neocortex, where it will be tagged as a *past*, no longer threatening event.

Unless this happens the trauma victim could have a whole lifetime of living in the past. And when the past is terrifying, their whole life is affected.

Some therapeutic methods are quite effective, though.

Resurrected hypnosis and tapping

A couple of techniques have had some success in treating PTSD.

In eye movement desensitization reprocessing (EMDR), the traumatized person recalls the traumatic event while focusing their eyes on the side to side hand movements of the therapist. Sometimes the process is automated with a moving light.

This is clearly a resurrected version of the old watch-swinging hypnotic induction. Its practitioners seem to be at a loss to explain why it can be effective.[4] But we can see that by keeping part of the client's attention in the present time (by having them concentrate on something that is happening *now*) while recalling the traumatic memory, their brain has a chance to assess the terrifying memory more objectively, and, we hope, log it as 'past', releasing it from the amygdala and instead storing it in the neocortex where it belongs.

The emotional freedom technique (EFT) is similar to EMDR in that it also aims to split the traumatized person's attention – this time, by 'tapping' them. Traditionally this 'tapping' has applied to 'meridian points' on the body and is claimed to release 'blocked energy channels' that cause negative emotions. This claim has no scientific basis.

But that is not to say that the technique is completely without merit. If we look to recent brain research (as opposed to ancient Eastern philosophy!), we can see that 'tapping' someone while they are recalling a traumatic event will also keep 'jogging' them back to the here and now, escaping the emotional response pattern encoded in the amygdala and giving the brain a chance to re-tag the terrifying event as distinct from *now*, and therefore as *past*.

When people have uncontrolled flashbacks they tend to lose contact with the present moment and become totally immersed in the past event. Tapping them, or having them follow an object from side to side, stops that happening. The amygdala gets a chance to 'give up' the memory to the neocortex, where it can finally be properly tagged as past, and no longer a threat.

Both these methods can be effective, but both run the risk of severe client distress, and neither is as thorough, comfortable, or effective as the Rewind Technique.

Further, if you don't fully understand the principles of what you are doing, and are relying on a 'formula', you will tend to be less adaptive and responsive to the unique needs of your client.

So what is the Rewind Technique, and why do I think all therapists need to know how to use it?

Be kind: Rewind

The origins of Rewind lie in Dr. Milton Erickson's 'Crystal Ball' technique. Erickson would hypnotize traumatized clients and have them review their traumatic time 'in a crystal ball', while feeling calm. If a memory is recalled in a state of calm even *once*, this can be enough to decondition the trauma.

The principle was further developed by Richard Bandler and John Grinder of NLP fame, and clumsily titled the visual-kinesthetic dissociation (VKD) technique. Dr. David Muss developed the technique so that it could be effectively used in the treatment of PTSD, and called it 'the Rewind Technique'.

Further refined and promoted widely in recent years by The Human Givens Institute, the Rewind Technique is now a highly effective method for a traumatized client to review their memories from an entirely dissociated, relaxed perspective. [5]

The traumatic event is experienced 'in reverse'. This is such an unusual way of processing the memory that the amygdala doesn't recognize it. The *fear* element is absent: nobody has a fear of things that happen in reverse.

Using this method is almost always entirely comfortable for clients. I myself have used it for survivors of torture, car and train crashes, attempted murder, and, of course, rape. It's also effective for the treatment of many phobias – in fact, I used the Rewind on myself many years ago to successfully overcome a fear of public speaking.[6]

And what about June?

The upshot for June

It's easy to think, when you hear June's story, "Oh, how awful for her!" But try for a moment to imagine the reality of being terrorized day and night by your own mind... for years.

Imagine trying to 'act normal' day after day, while feeling your life could be ripped from you any second. That is the reality for millions of PTSD sufferers. There is nothing 'theoretical' or 'abstract' about PTSD when you're the one living the nightmare.

I can't tell you how many times I've completed a session of Rewind and been told, "That memory feels quite distant now" or "It's like it doesn't matter anymore."

I used Rewind with June for her worst memories of rape. Although she'd been raped hundreds of times, we found that, once the worst dozen or so memories had been detraumatized, there was a kind of snowball effect, and her brain learned the new pattern and all the trauma went.

And then something weird happened. Weird for June, anyway!

A new life

As June recovered, she started regularly sleeping through the night – something she couldn't ever remember doing. She enrolled in a training course and got a new, more rewarding job. She ended her unhealthy relationship and found a man she could love and be loved by. The flashbacks stopped completely.

As her body started to let go of the stress, she even started to look younger.

"I'm here to be alive, not just survive," she said.

She is such a decent, brave, kind person. It was an honor to help her.

Near the end of our sessions, she made an announcement.

Confronting demons

"There's going to be a family wedding," she told me. "My uncle will be there. I want to go. But even though he's nearly 80 now, I still feel that somehow he might have power over me, that it could all happen again."

This would be a real test. She hadn't seen this man in over thirty years!

We hypnotically rehearsed her feeling relaxed and calm during the upcoming wedding. The next (and last) time I saw her, she told me that the wedding had gone really well. Her uncle had been there, as expected, but his presence had no effect on her.

"He was just so small and insignificant. Just nothing to me. Just part of a forgotten life I lived centuries ago. It's time for me to live properly now and not in the past."

And she is doing just that.

So if you treat trauma (and if not, why not?), I urge you to avoid any method that relies on getting your client to 'relive' past horrors as they occurred.

Your traumatized client has had enough pain in their life; they don't need to pay you to have more.

It's appalling to me that there are still therapists, counsellors, and doctors out there who don't know how to effectively treat trauma.

Millions of people are suffering needlessly. It needs to stop.

SIX

WHY I NEVER HAVE MY CLIENTS RELIVE THEIR TRAUMATIC EXPERIENCES

WHY 'TALKING THROUGH THE TRAUMA' ONLY EMBEDS IT

"I was there, in that kitchen. Thirty-five years just dropped away, like armor come loose, leaving me naked and weak. University, my first job, my marriage, my adulthood, all gone, because I was now in the past. I was twelve; home from school on that day. I saw it as if I was right there again. Not a memory, a reliving.

"The second I saw my mum hanging there, I knew she was dead. That second, the longest and the shortest of my life. That second, that stretched out into so many years of depression and pain. I tried and tried to get her down, I started screaming, just as I had when I was twelve; I couldn't stop crying. It's no good. I can't forget, I just can't, even after all this time!"

The tone of his voice told me this was a man long accustomed to wrestling down tears. It took a while before he could fight down his heartache enough to speak, and when he did, he spoke very quickly, as if desperate to get it all out before it overwhelmed him.

Colin was one of several clients I've met over the years who had been deeply traumatized by the horror of discovering the body of a loved one after suicide. He told me all about 'the evil time machine'.

'Help' can sometimes harm

You see, before he came to see me, Colin had been to a therapist whose treatment approach was based on the maxim that in order to help heal trauma you have to relive it, and re-experience all the original feelings again as they happened.

That therapist also believed that many traumas are hidden, blocked out by the conscious mind, and need to be 'uncovered' and then relived through the imagination. He believed that in order to 'let it go', Colin needed to 'get in touch with' all the raw pain and emotions of the traumas he'd experienced.

This therapeutic myth has been around for over a century.

At the Tavistock Clinic, London, in the 1920s, getting patients to relive their war traumas was regarded as the gold standard in the treatment of trauma – or 'hysteria', as it was known at the time. There were apparently no boundaries when it came to achieving this aim. Horrifically traumatized victims of bomb explosions were covered in mud all over again, all in the name of 'treatment'.

The aim was to produce psychological 'collapse' through the reliving of the ordeal. But we now know that any improvement that patients experienced was brought about not through the horrific reliving of the trauma but through the sense of calm that came with complete emotional exhaustion *after* the 'collapse'.

We can help people access the traumatic memory by

helping them dissociate from it calmly, so that all bad feelings can be avoided.

Therapy should never be painful.

With this in mind...

Three reasons I never get a client to directly relive their traumatic experiences

Reason One: You can reactivate the pattern and embed it deeper

In the last article, I made reference to a quote from psychologist Dr. Noreen Tehrani, who specializes in post-traumatic stress. It's worth repeating here:

> *"If a trauma victim is debriefed in a state of high emotion, the process can increase the arousal to the point of overload, trapping the sensory impressions in the amygdala."*

This is why 'critical incident debriefing' after traumatic events is falling out of favor. Not only does getting people to talk about trauma while they are traumatized not help, it could actually make things worse.[1]

Getting people to 'relive' their trauma is not therapy. But it can be torture.

Reason Two: Someone who desperately needs help may be put off ever seeking it

I was amazed that Colin still wanted anything to do with any therapy after what he'd been through with the therapist he'd seen before me. I did my best to undo the damage done by the outdated treatment he'd received (in itself almost as traumatic as his initial tragic experience).

If you don't know how to detraumatize someone comfortably, then at least avoid hurting them and/or putting them off seeking help in future.

Reason Three: It's a waste of valuable time

If you're going the wrong way, it doesn't matter how fast you're travelling. You are still wasting time.

People who are suffering flashbacks, experiencing terror day and night, living the kind of life no one should have to live, becoming depressed, perhaps falling into substance abuse, damaging their relationships, watching their careers fall apart, and all the rest of it, need help *right now*.

By all means, if you hold with that particular ideology, do as much long-term 'deep' stuff with your client (if they don't mind and have the money) as you want. But please – remove their traumatic suffering as fast as you can, and preferably in the first session.

Rocking the boat?

Some therapists have told me that therapeutic practice should be a 'matter of choice' for the therapist, as if methods of alleviating human suffering are a question of 'taste', like what movies appeal to us, or what we feel to be good art.

Would you say that hygienic practice in maternity wards should be a 'matter of choice'? In the sixteenth and seventeenth centuries, promoters of hand washing were derided for suggesting it was better practice to have a clean environment rather than a dirty one.[2] Opponents of 'germ theory' thought it unfair that anyone should see fit to criticize their filthy operating theaters, or suggest that they ought to wash their hands between patients.

Centuries later, this seems so ridiculous it's almost funny. A century from now, I hope therapists look back at critical incident debriefing with the same bemusement. Relieving trauma comfortably and quickly is simply best practice. There is no 'matter of choice' about it.

Colin no longer has flashbacks, either to the trauma of finding his mother dead or to the therapy that nearly broke him. He has moved on comfortably and happily told me, "I never have to relive it again!"

SEVEN

WHY PTSD AND PHOBIAS ARE A CASE OF BAD HYPNOSIS

HOW POST-HYPNOTIC SUGGESTIONS WORK IN EMOTIONAL PROBLEMS

Hypnotherapists will often describe hypnosis as 'a state of relaxation similar to daydreaming', presumably to reassure and encourage people to try hypnotherapy. This is correct in that therapeutic hypnosis should be relaxing (as well as energizing).

But not all hypnosis is good, and some of it can be very bad indeed.

Learning and your unconscious mind

Hypnosis is a state of tightly narrowed focus of attention, a state in which we become better at learning because this narrowing of focus makes us more 'suggestible'. The *kind* of learning we do in natural (as well as therapeutically induced) hypnotic states tends to be *unconscious* learning – we learn, but are not aware that we are doing so. But conscious learning also takes place in hypnotic states.

Whatever you have *really* learnt in life, you learnt in a state of *trance*. Whether it was good or bad, whether you were learning consciously or unconsciously, your attention was *narrowly focused* on the learning, and certain elements of reality were *excluded*.

Bad hypnosis = bad (but very effective) learning

The negative emotional states of depression, anger, addiction, and fear are all hypnotic. They require narrowed focus in order to persist, and will often exclude from our attention those aspects of reality that contradict the 'symptomatic trance state'.

All strong emotional trance states make people more suggestible, just like the more familiar therapeutic (or even stage show) trance states. In traumatized clients, if we know what to look for, we can clearly see classic post-hypnotic responses in operation.

Post-hypnotic stress disorder

A woman attending a stage hypnosis show is selected as one of the show's 'stars' because she is an excellent hypnotic subject. While deeply hypnotized, she is given the suggestion that, after she has come out of trance, she will, on hearing the hypnotist say the word 'rhubarb', tip back into a wide awake hypnotic trance and believe she is Marilyn Monroe. This is a classic post-hypnotic suggestion. She comes out of trance, and some time later the hypnotist shouts "Rhubarb!" And *before she knows it* she is acting out and believing she's the great screen blond bombshell.

A man walks across a bridge and his attention is suddenly deeply and tightly focused on the muggers who accost him. He believes he is going to die. He is threatened with a knife to his throat, hypnotized by the situation. He is robbed, but left unharmed. The following week he tries to cross a similar bridge but *before he knows it* finds himself reaching the same level of panic as when he was attacked, even though this time he is quite safe and with friends.

In this second case we can clearly see how the post-traumatic stress response is not a result of *thinking* but of deep *emotional conditioning*. His narrowed attention during the attack delivered the hypnotic 'suggestion' that bridges are dangerous places and, until he is cured, bridges will continue to produce a post-hypnotic response in this man.

Trauma and hypnotic response

All post-traumatic stress disorder produces very real post-hypnotic responses in the sufferer, to the extent that some people feel as if they are right back in the original trauma, hearing, feeling, seeing and smelling everything from the original time, just as if it was *actually happening now*.

This level of 'wide awake dreaming' is just what we see in stage hypnosis subjects. Mainstream psychology hasn't yet linked PTSD or phobic responses to the mechanism of post-hypnotic response, but it will do so eventually. And in fact research has found that people suffering long term post-traumatic stress disorder are also people who are better at responding to hypnosis.[1]

So what does this mean for us therapists?

Treat bad hypnosis with good hypnosis

It makes sense to use hypnosis to treat a 'hypnotic disorder'. Trying to treat trauma by getting people to 'think differently' (as in cognitive therapy) is often cumbersome and ineffective, because there is no problem with the way a PTSD sufferer *thinks*. The man crossing the bridge *knows* he will probably not be mugged again – but that doesn't stop his panic response.

Treating at the level of conscious cognition is a mistake – we need to treat the subconscious conditioning that causes the response.

As we learned earlier, there are two longstanding methods of trauma treatment that are essentially hypnotic in nature (even if they were developed without that realization!). Eye movement desensitization and reprocessing (EMDR) and the emotional freedom technique (EFT) focus the subject's attention using a moving object and touch respectively, as a way of accessing the hypnotic REM state.

But in my opinion the Rewind Technique is the real crème de la crème of trauma treatment. Applying all the principles of comfortable and enduring relief, this approach uses hypnotically dissociated memory reprocessing to put a complete stop to post-traumatic stress.

Fast, safe, effective and life-changing – it's the perfect example of 'good hypnosis'.

EIGHT

IS TRAUMA LOCKING YOUR CLIENT IN DEPRESSION?

WHY LIFTING A TRAUMATIC MEMORY BRINGS RAPID PROGRESS IN YOUR DEPRESSED CLIENT

"It doesn't make sense. I have everything to live for! I have a wonderful boyfriend, a great job, lovely friends, but I've started feeling really afraid... no, more than that, actually terrified. I've been signed off work with 'stress' and I've stopped going out at all. I just want to stay at home, with the door bolted. It seems like I can't escape these feelings. I'm starting to feel as though I have nothing to live for... and that's just not true."

Sam was deeply depressed when she came to see me. She seemed shot through with sadness. Tears began to moisten her eyes.

"How long have you been feeling depressed, Sam?"

"I think it's about three months now."

"Did anything happen around three months ago, anything that was out of the ordinary for you?"

Sam's brow furrowed with the effort of thinking back across the miserable weeks.

"Well, I was involved in a minor car accident around then. But it really wasn't anything serious. I just dented my car in a parking lot. Silly thing to do."

"And it was after that that you started to feel anxious and then depressed?"

"Yes."

"And had you ever been in any other kind of car crash before that minor incident in the parking lot three months ago?"

A shadow crossed her face as I put this question to her. She suddenly looked older, weighed down by some invisible burden.

"Yes, I have. Ten years ago, I was quite badly burned in a car crash, mainly my legs. I was trapped and lost consciousness. I don't remember being hauled out of the car. The driver, my boyfriend, was killed."

She paused, and then said in a small voice,

"But that was so long ago..."

"Now, Sam this little collision you had a few months back... how did it affect you?"

"Well, I was surprised, really. I found myself crying about it afterwards, and felt really badly shaken up, even though nothing serious had happened. I started having nightmares about that time again, like I had for years after my boyfriend died."

We talked about this some more, and Sam agreed that it was possible that the very minor collision she'd had (in which her car had been only slightly scratched at low speed) may have reactivated traumatic feelings around the decade old trauma.

I decided to go for the trauma 'litmus test'.

"Sam, when you recall the crash from ten years ago now,

does it make you feel frightened in the here and now to remember it...? Just do that for a few seconds... just recall that old crash."

Sam turned pale and began to tremble. I quickly encouraged her to refocus her attention on me and 'come out of it'. I am not in the business of making my clients feel anxious.

Sam told me that the memory felt as fresh as if it was from yesterday, and that she was 'right back there again' whenever she thought about that crash or anything reminded her of it.

It seemed to me there was no other reason why Sam could have become depressed.

Her emotional and physical needs were being met, she had not been particularly worried about anything, and then, after a minor scrape in her car, her life started to fall apart.

Three reasons why unresolved trauma may tip someone into clinical depression.

One: High stress levels

Depression rides off the back of anxiety and stress.

All depressed people are pumped so full of the stress hormone cortisol that eventually they become exhausted, and feel hopeless and powerless. Without heightened stress levels in the body, there can be no depression.[1]

Sustained or chronic stress leads to:

- elevated levels of cortisol (the 'stress hormone'), and
- reduced levels of serotonin and dopamine (the 'feel good' chemicals) and other neurotransmitters in the brain.

Unmanaged stress, particularly unresolved trauma, blocks the action of these chemicals, which regulate vital biological processes from sleep and energy to sex drive and appetite, and also permit expression of normal moods and emotions.

When the stress response fails to shut off and reset after a difficult situation has passed, it can lead to depression in susceptible people.

All depression treatment needs to include relaxation training to help people bring down their stress levels.

But feeling traumatized also results in another phenomenon that is often a key factor in depression.

Two: Feeling helpless

People can survive any deprivation or stress if they feel they can *surmount it*. It's when people feel helpless that they feel hopeless.

We all need to feel we have some control over at least some parts of our lives. So feeling that we have no control, and are powerless and helpless, is hugely depressing.

'Learned helplessness' (*feeling* helpless when you're not, because you were helpless in the past) is a major feature of many depressions. This kind of learning makes people more susceptible to depression, and learned helplessness may have to be specifically 'unlearned' in treatment.

When people are traumatized, their *emotions* also feel totally out of control. For all those years following that tragic crash, Sam would have felt emotionally vulnerable as different elements of life 'pattern matched' to her original trauma, and made her feel powerless again. She hadn't spotted this consciously, but the unresolved trauma made her more susceptible to depression.

Three: Unfulfilled needs

Human beings become depressed when

- their innate human needs remain unmet over a long period, and
- they ruminate negatively about the hopelessness of those needs ever being met, thus racking up their stress levels even higher.

If this situation continues long enough, people become emotionally and physically exhausted.[2]

We all need to:

- feel safe and secure day to day
- give and receive attention
- have a sense of control and influence over events in our lives
- feel stretched and stimulated by life to avoid boredom
- have fun sometimes and feel life is enjoyable
- feel intimate with at least one other human being
- feel connected to and part of a wider community
- have some privacy and time to privately reflect
- have a recognizable and appreciated role in life
- have a sense of competence and achievement
- have a sense of meaning about life and what we do.[3]

Continuing to be traumatized long after a distressing event makes us feel powerless and avoidant. But if we start to avoid things that might actually help us to meet our innate needs, such as company, intimacy, or fun, we are at increased risk of depression.

This is how trauma can block the completion of these needs and both cause and maintain depression.

It's not *always* about trauma

People depress for all kinds of reasons, and we should never assume that unresolved trauma must be a cause. Going off looking for 'traumas' that just aren't there can make 'therapy' quite toxic for depressed people whose depression has a different cause.

However, trauma *is* sometimes a major factor in depression, which is why it is vital that all therapists know how to:

- *correctly identify* trauma, and
- *relieve* it fast.

After I used the Rewind Technique with Sam, she was able to think about the crash from ten years before while feeling quite calm. She said to me:

"I'm sad about what happened, but I'm so glad to finally feel like it's properly in the past."

Sam's depression lifted almost as fast as it had begun, as the heightened stress caused by the reactivation of the previously unresolved trauma was no longer there to maintain the depression. She started going out again, went back to work a few days later, felt safe at last and started having the life she should have had all along.

NINE

HELPING YOUR CLIENT READJUST TO LIFE AFTER TRAUMA

COMMON PROBLEMS FACING THOSE RECENTLY DETRAUMATIZED

The terror in your client's mind isn't hard to ease. PTSD can be lifted in a single session, especially if it springs from a one-off incident.

But once you've lifted your client's flashbacks and nightmares, you might still have to work hard at helping them adjust to a life *without* fear.

My friend and colleague Dan Jones once told me how he had helped a woman who had been (literally) imprisoned in her home by her own fear for twenty years. Following two traumatic events, her panic attacks became so bad that in 1985 she stopped going out altogether.

It wasn't until two torturous decades later that Dan arrived on the scene. Using the Rewind Technique, he was able to finally detraumatize the unfortunate woman. That very same day, they headed down to the seafront together and sat on a bench eating ice cream. Just like that, she was free at last. No more fear!

But, like Rip Van Winkle waking up after his twenty year snooze, she found that the world had changed.

People behaved differently in the street – walking along, chins on chests, tapping furiously into cell phones. People looked different – acres of tattooed skin on show, all those piercings. When you've been trapped in 1985, the relentless rush of 2005 life takes some getting used to. Just as eyes have to adapt after years in darkness, so too does the mind need to adjust to a drastic change in the environment.

Not feeling afraid can take some getting used to.

A good problem to have, of course, but one the recently detraumatized might still need help with, especially if their trauma was longstanding.

Ideas to help you help your clients adjust to life beyond trauma.

1) Prepare them for freedom

Before getting down to deconditioning a traumatic memory (or memories), ask your client how they expect and hope their life to be different once they are no longer traumatized.

This question might seem impossibly abstract to them, because PTSD sufferers often don't really believe it can be lifted until it has been. But it can help them prepare for wellness.

You might ask questions like:

- How is your daily life going to change once the flashbacks of that assault have stopped?
- What are you going to be able to do that you haven't been able to do up to now, once that trauma has been put behind you?
- How are your relationships going to be different

once these memories have begun to feel distant and non-threatening?

Have you heard of the 'butterfly effect'?

This expression comes from the development of 'chaos theory', and refers to the way one tiny change (a butterfly flapping its wings in Brazil) inevitably changes the *whole of reality* in unseen but sometimes dramatic ways –leading to the emergence of a tornado elsewhere, for example. Change one part of a system and other parts will also *inevitably* change.

Curing someone of a life-blighting trauma is not a small change, and the cure *will* produce changes and benefits in sometimes quite unexpected ways. As far as possible you can prepare for that.

And you can do this specifically.

2) Rehearse the changes

Once you have detraumatized your client, and while they are deeply relaxed, have them mentally rehearse inwardly experiencing (not just thinking about) the changes they told you they expected to experience once the trauma was lifted.

For example, one man who had been badly beaten up in a bar while abroad was unable to go out socially afterwards because of his fear. When I asked him how his life would be different after his fear had gone, he told me (rather wistfully, as he was still doubtful that I really could help him) that he would just love to be able to go for a drink with his two best friends again.

After using the Rewind Technique with him, and while he was still in a state of deep relaxation, I got him to vividly mentally rehearse being out having fun with his two friends in various pubs and bars that they liked to frequent.

Not only that, but we also mentally rehearsed him calling up his friends to suggest meeting up for a drink, getting ready to go out, travelling to the venue and so on. This helped to make the totality of the experience feel natural and normal for him.

3) Get practical!

I once helped a guy overcome a severe phobia of travelling on trains. Right then and there (we happened to be right next door to a railway station, which helped!) we went out after the session and got on a train. He was fine.

Dan went out with the woman he helped release not just from the terror of her own mind but from the captivity of her house.

If it's practical to do so, be with your client when they take their first steps away from trauma or phobia.

When lifting PTSD from war veterans, the overcoming of the PTSD itself is of course the vital and massive first step, but we can also help them reintegrate back into civilian life, and in other ways too. And the same is true for anyone who has lived with their trauma for any length of time.

TEN

ENCOURAGING POST-TRAUMATIC GROWTH IN YOUR CLIENT

GENTLE WAYS TO HELP YOUR CLIENT LOOK BACK POSITIVELY AT THE PAST

"Every adversity, every failure, every heartache carries with it the seed of an equal or greater benefit."

NAPOLEON HILL

We all hear so much about the *bad* effects of suffering, but as therapists (and human beings!), we would do well to remember the opportunities for growth that personal adversity can offer. We should never deny or downplay the impact of suffering, but *part* of the impact may be personal growth, and we shouldn't deny that either.

We can help clients to experience post-traumatic growth and feel better about their lives by establishing a sense of benefit (however hard that might be at first) from their current or past trials.

Which reminds me of the story of a certain beggar...

The King's Beggar

Once upon a time there lived a downtrodden beggar, nothing to the world and easily forgotten. Yet through sheer unstinting effort, sprinkled with a good measure of luck, he rose in life to become a trusted advisor to the king. And such were his honesty and wisdom that he soon secured a place smack bang in the heart of the king's affections. But as everyone knows, favorites attract resentment, and a jealous tide began to swell.

The advisors whom the new man had displaced began a poisonous whisper plot to sabotage his position. They spied on 'the king's beggar', as they disparagingly dubbed him, to see if they could find a way to catch him out. Their luck was in. Every night, in his wonderfully furnished apartment in the palace, they watched him go into a certain antechamber, where he would remove some bricks from the wall, and then stare at something he was obviously hoarding there. Very suspicious!

Soon, like viperous smoke, their evil insinuations sinuously crept their way into the king's ear. They more than hinted that there was 'evidence' that the king's favorite was stealing the royal wealth, hoarding it away, and gazing at it with glee each night. The king would hear none of it ... at first.

But then the sparks of doubt, fanned as they were by the jealous courtiers, took hold and were soon burning wildly in the royal heart. How could this favorite whom he had trusted so much have so deceived him? At last, one night the king could bear it no more. He strode into the luxurious apartment he had himself given to the man who had once been a penniless beggar, and confronted him.

The king roared, "I have it on trusted authority that you have been stealing from my royal treasure chests and each night gaze upon you ill-gotten gains! I command you to open up the secret compartment in your wall and show me what you've been stealing from me!"

"Very well," said the erstwhile beggar calmly, "but what you see may surprise Your Majesty."

"Just do it!"

So the one-time beggar prized certain loose bricks out of the wall and revealed ... a pair of the most tattered and dirty old shoes the king had ever seen.

Relieved to find no stolen treasure, His Majesty was still perplexed.

"Why do you come here each night to stare at a pair of worn-out old shoes?" he demanded.

The former beggar looked at the king with level eyes and said, "Because it is not despite having come from beggarly beginnings that I am able to fulfill my duties for Your Majesty, but because I was once a beggar.

"Begging taught me the true value of patience, faith, trust, and hard work, and the inner value of people over outer appearances. The time in my life from which these poor broken sandals come taught me to see people clearly, to see both their generosities and meannesses, to have resilience, but also strategy.

"I look at these sandals every day to remind myself where I came from, where I could so easily go back to. These beggars' sandals are the most important thing that have ever happened to me, more than wealth and position, because ... they taught me how to be, and that, whatever happens, I can survive."

At these words the king shed tears at how easily he had been led to doubt his 'royal beggar'.

Learning from the tough times

We seldom now talk about 'character' and how character is built or strengthened through experience. We are more likely to talk of how adverse experiences weaken.

Experiences, like commercial commodities, are seen as desirable or undesirable rather than as toughening, or as opportunity for the development of wisdom.

This is a great shame, and we disserve our clients if we 'steal' any sense of the good that bad experiences can bring.

Human emotional distress has been so pathologized and medicalized that it has come to be seen as something that should be eradicated altogether. But if we really can only gain certain kinds of wisdom from adversity, then the (impossible) aspiration for us all to be 'happy' all the time might actually be having a weakening effect on the human race. Clients can come to feel ashamed of previous episodes of depression, or even of having had disadvantaged childhoods, as if any admission of not being perfect and 'normal' is blameworthy.

The *meaning* people place upon their experiences determines how empowered or disempowered they feel with regard to their personal history. The worst scenario is when someone feels they are 'damaged goods', unequal, inferior, because of what happened to them in the past. It's important to think in an 'antifragile' way sometimes.

The power of antifragile

The writer Nassim Taleb coined the term 'antifragile' to describe someone who is not just *resilient* to a stressor but actually *benefits* from it.[1] Wolff's Law states that bones are not just resilient to the stress of weight bearing but *strengthened* by it (up to a point, of course).[2] Street kids in Mumbai learn to live by their wits, think strategically, and maintain hope against all odds – these are *strengths* from adversity. Of course, when the adversity becomes too much it may *overwhelm* us – but even that weakening effect may only be temporary, as the person pushes through it and resumes *gaining* in strength.

It's vital to help our clients lift depression, overcome addiction and PTSD, and so on, but at the same time we can help clients focus not just on what they've lost through disadvantaged pasts but what they may also have gained in some way.

We're not trying to convince people that the trauma or hardships they endured were actually a good thing, but rather that they carry some kind of learning 'nutrition' that can be helpful and strengthening and may not become active until long after the events.

This can help people feel more confident, less like 'damaged goods'.

To that end...

Three therapy strategies to help your clients benefit from 'post-traumatic growth'.

1) What did they learn?

You sometimes hear people say things like "If only that hadn't happened!" or "Why do bad things happen to good people?" Perhaps it is so we can learn.

I sometimes talk to my traumatized clients about 'post-traumatic growth'. I do this only *after* we have stopped flashbacks and nightmares, of course, because otherwise it would seem like trying to put a positive spin on what still *feels* too awful. Ask your client what they have learned about life and themselves from their experiences. If you have deconditioned a trauma with the Rewind Technique, you might ask your client to consider both what they learned from the trauma itself and what they can now learn from overcoming it.

For example, if someone has felt intense fear and flashbacks from an event that occurred twenty years ago, but no longer does so after your treatment, then they've learnt that what felt stuck and immovable *wasn't* stuck and immovable, and that everything *can* improve even when it feels like it never can. This is a massive learning experience. If you've had PTSD removed, for the rest of your life you'll be grateful for each 'normal' day.

If someone was depressed for a long time, the 'lesson' from that might be that they now know clearly what their emotional needs really are and can respect themselves enough to meet those needs better in future.

"Why did that have to happen to me?" can transform into "What did I learn from that time or those experiences that has made or could make me stronger?"

As with most things, timing is vital. For someone who's just come through your door wanting to tell you their woes, asking what they have learnt from their adversities might break rapport at the very moment when they need you just to listen. But *along with* other interventions, the "What have you learned?'" question can help find meaning in the meaningless.

2) Talk about powerful crux points

"...failure meant a stripping away of the inessential. I stopped pretending to myself that I was anything other than what I was, and began to direct all my energy into finishing the only work that mattered to me."

J. K. ROWLING ON THE BENEFITS OF FAILURE

It is during a crisis that we really learn what is important to us, what really matters. As we just discussed, we can talk to our clients about how adversities of all kinds can lead to opportunities for growth as the desperate 'something has to change' crux point is reached.

All fear is about expectation of loss. When you feel you have *already* lost and there is now *nothing to lose* then, strangely, fear can subside and real gains can be made.

A friend of mine described how years ago she'd had a terrible fear of flying. But she heard her mother was deathly ill and needed to take a flight to be with her. She made that flight through a tremendous storm but amazingly felt no fear. "Nothing mattered to me anymore except that I got to see my mother ..."

One client drew a blank when I asked him what his latest depressive crux point had enabled him to do, until he suddenly said, "Well, I became so desperate I thought I would try hypnotherapy. So I have come to you for help!" A backhanded compliment, to be sure, but it illustrates that necessity is the mother of invention, and so is desperation. And from desperation stems growth.

3) Use metaphor to encourage post-traumatic growth

I've suggested these before, but I make no excuse for repeating myself here, because they work so well.

I might talk to a client (in or out of hypnotic trance) about how it is the stone that is thrashed around in the sea that ends up the most beautifully polished. Or to someone who suffered adversity as a child I might talk about the oak tree that becomes tall and strong, weathering the storms, and ends up with the most interesting appearance, big enough and strong enough to provide shelter for animals and birds, not at all like those spoiled over protected trees that just grow up boringly straight, protected by plastic cones..."

Again I would emphasize that the aim is not to convince our clients that what happened to them was 'good'. We just want to help them, where appropriate, feel they can benefit *in some way* from what happened to them, to use the 'roughage of life' (as Dr. Milton Erickson called problems) to provide some kind of nutrition for them in the form of better judgment, more wisdom, or resilience in the present and future.

When people are depressed, anxious, jealous, or angry, they use their own imaginations against their own (and other people's) best interests. By using therapeutic metaphors we help people use their imaginations *constructively*.

We might even tell someone the story of 'the king's beggar' when it comes to helping people grow, not in spite of but *because* of their past – however bad it was.

ELEVEN

HOW TO MAXIMIZE CLIENT COMFORT WHEN USING THE WORLD'S MOST EFFECTIVE PTSD CURE

3 SPECIFIC PROTECTIVE LANGUAGE TECHNIQUES TO USE WHEN TREATING PTSD AND PHOBIAS

The air in the room seemed to crackle with urgency as he spoke.

His eyes were wide, fixed in a gaze of eternal horror; an unfading snapshot of an unbearable moment continually lived.

James only alluded to the severe physical and sexual abuse he'd suffered – he couldn't bring himself to describe it directly.

The old 'sticks and stones' adage couldn't be further from the truth. Words can hurt, even when they come from our own mouth.

It wasn't just that he had suffered abuse, but that he was still living that horror. Many years later, the now he lived in was still that same now he'd experienced back then.

Trauma locks people in time. No matter how hard they try to move forward, it keeps them anchored in the past, like a fiend yanking them back by the throat.

But there was something else James said that really got to me.

Treating trauma: First do no harm

The post-traumatic stress James was suffering from childhood abuse had gotten worse after seeing a particular therapist. Finally, in his 30s, he'd mustered the courage to seek help for his terrible nightmares and flashbacks – and all he got was more pain and muddled therapeutic theory.

"He made me talk about what happened. He even made me close my eyes and try to relive it. He seemed to think that was the key to getting better. He told me there must be something that I didn't remember that was the real root of my PTSD! But I *already* knew what caused it. I *already* remembered it, only too well!"

James now had terrible memories not just of the abuse, but of *the therapy itself*. His nightmares and flashbacks got worse. He dreaded every session, and needed time just to recover after each one.

James's therapist tried to convince him that all this extra pain was somehow "part of the healing process". Clearly, he had a severely limited knowledge as to what trauma actually is.

Amazingly, James was still prepared to give therapy another go. "I felt there had to be help out there for me", he explained. And he wasn't wrong.

EMDR & EFT: Flicking eyes and tapping fingers

James's next therapist tried Eye Movement Desensitization Reprocessing (EMDR) and the Emotional Freedom Technique (EFT), or 'tapping'. James found this a bit more useful (which wasn't hard after his first experience!), and it seemed to help him at least get back to where he was before seeing the first therapist.

But it wasn't coupled with deep relaxation, and the howling nightmares continued.

Still James found himself plagued by the memories. The distraction of self-tapping during a flashback would sometimes help it pass a little quicker – when he remembered to do it – but it wasn't enough.

When we truly understand what trauma is and what is needed to lift it, only then can we offer real hope and help.

So what does a traumatized client really need?

To help a client overcome trauma, we need to keep them:

1. Comfortable and relaxed.
2. Present: PTSD drags people back in time, or at least that's the way it feels.
3. Disassociated: The client needs to experience being associated with the present or a sense of resourceful empowerment, and disassociated from the trauma itself. When this happens even decades old trauma can be lifted incredibly comfortably and fast.

Any technique that can help clients do these three things will help them.

Trying to get clients who are less extremely traumatized to talk through what happened may help them process the trauma eventually, but it could be painful. And for around a quarter of clients [(1)], talking about the trauma will actually deepen it, because it means they have to experience the horror again and again.

This knowledge has been available for some time, and I feel it is unethical to continue to try to treat trauma in ways that do not take the nature of trauma and trauma cure into account.

The Rewind technique is currently the most comfortable

and reliable way of using the three principles of ethical trauma resolution. It's an amazingly quick and safe way to lift debilitating trauma or phobias.

But even when using Rewind, practitioners still need to consider the way they communicate. The *language* you use when working with Rewind can make all the difference to both its effectiveness and your client's comfort.

Just as you must avoid peanuts if you have a nut allergy or gluten if you're coeliac, you must avoid provocative language if you're treating someone with trauma. Keeping our language safe, at least until the trauma or phobia is lifted, is paramount.

Avoiding hair triggers

Phobic or traumatized people often find that the slightest trigger 'sets them off'. And words can be powerful triggers. Just the mention of the word 'spider' can spark terror in an arachnophobe. I've found the word 'rape' or 'assault' or even 'memory' can *automatically* arouse the severely traumatized or phobic person.

I worked with a car crash survivor whose partner had died in the crash. She herself hadn't been seriously physically injured, but she was acutely traumatized. Until the trauma was lifted, she couldn't hear the word 'car' or 'crash' without her body flooding with adrenaline. Such is the immense power of pattern matching.

In one of my workshops, I cured a woman of a belly button phobia. Before we worked together she couldn't say or hear the word 'belly button', and she had her own 'BB' as she called it taped over so she couldn't see it. After a single Rewind session, she could say it easily. In fact, she took great delight in doing so over and over!

For the Rewind technique to be effective, we want the

client to remain calm and relaxed throughout the session. But how can we deal with such specific scary memories *without* using potential 'trigger words'? I want to give you three protective language strategies that do just that.

1. Use 'code words'

Your client knows what happened to traumatize them, and they don't need you to retell them. Some very simple 'code words' can let them know what we're talking about without bringing up the specifics of the situation.

So when you Rewind a specific terrifying spider memory, don't talk about "the time when you were terrified by that big hairy spider jumping on your head from the grandfather clock". Simply refer to "that wooden clock time".

No 'terror', no 'spiders', no 'jumping'. I don't have to use these words for them to know what I'm talking about. Similarly, the 'code' for a car crash might simply be: "That time in December".

Lifting trauma is all about widening the emotional context. This can be quite straightforward if someone 'only' has a subthreshold trauma, but we can also help the process along with our use of language when applying Rewind.

The wooden clock or the fact it was December is a context that isn't the usual focus of a flashback, so this kind of language can help contextualize the memory and protect the person whilst the memory is being reprocessed as emotionally past and therefore safe.

2. Reframe a 'memory' as a 'video'

Traumatized and phobic people are plagued by their memories, so even just using the word 'memory' can provoke anxiety. But we can encourage disassociation from a traumatic memory during Rewind by describing it as "that out of date video". A memory is part of a person, but a video is outside of them. We can put it away and choose when or even if we play it.

The experience of watching an out of date video is very different from reliving a memory. Not only that, but watching something is also very distinct from feeling it, which implies being inside it. And as a final added bonus, the very concept of a video is now out of date!

3. Change tense to bring calm

Traumatic memories feel as if they are happening right now, even if the original trauma happened decades before. This is because the memory stays 'stuck' in the part of the brain that doesn't contextualize events as past. Cognitively, of course the person knows the horror isn't happening again each time it runs through their brain. But emotionally, it's another story.

After a Rewind session, clients typically report that the memory that had previously haunted them now feels distant. They may describe the memory as feeling like a long time ago, or like it can't affect them anymore.

We can encourage this sense of distance in time by emphasizing the past in what we talk about even as we apply Rewind. We can talk of "that *old, out-of-date* video *way back then...*" or "*that long-ago you* in that *ancient old video* way over there..."

But there's another great advantage to keeping our language safe before and after Rewind.

Testing our work

By *excluding* trigger words and *including* words that widen the context beyond horror as we work on the Rewind technique, we create a good 'test' to check that the trauma or phobia is now gone.

At the end of the session, we can reintroduce direct references to 'spiders' or 'the car crash' into the conversation. At this point we should see clear indications that these words are no longer triggers, and instead have become completely neutral words for the client. For some triggers, I take it a step further. I might use the word 'snake' first, then ask the client to actually see one.

The power of the Rewind technique is such that it is likely to work even when the practitioner doesn't specifically use these language tools – and many don't. But I believe we owe it to phobics and trauma survivors to make their recovery as comfortable as possible, and protective language really helps with that.

It makes me feel ashamed and embarrassed of my profession when I hear the stories of people like James, who seek help and end up feeling worse.

After his Rewind treatment, James said, and I'll never forget it:

"It feels like I can finally be me, like I'm no longer carrying that horrendous weight of terror and shame within me. I can connect with other people without this invisible wall of horror coming between us. I feel free, light, and happy."

As expected, James can now think about and, if he chooses, talk about what happened to him. But he doesn't need to. His nightmares have stopped, and the horror triggers that used to litter the landscape of his life no longer have any effect at all.

He is free.

TWELVE
TRAUMA AND REWIND TECHNIQUE Q&A

These are some examples of questions from students on my Rewind Technique course over the years. As part of the course, we conduct a live Q&A session online every month.

Student question:

During the rewind technique with a client that has had multiple traumas....do you do it for each trauma?

My answer:

It's great to hear you love our material and from someone who has trained at the Milton Erickson Foundation that's praise indeed!

I think as far as possible it's best to deal with one trauma at a time. Sometimes we work with someone who has been multiply abused over many years. I'm thinking of the woman I worked with who had been raped many hundreds of times over a six year period by her uncle.

The abuse only stopped when she ran away from home. Now even with someone with so many traumas there will be ones that stand out as particularly terrifying. So I asked her to indicate she had thought of the worst ones. I didn't have her tell me too much about them but she gave me code words which represented each time.

Now I saw her maybe seven times and during that time we rewound dozens of memories but also...it's a strange thing. It's as though the unconscious mind starts to do it for itself...so even ones we hadn't worked on she reported that the memories had been deconditioned. A kind of happy dominoes effect.

So rather than just rewinding a general sense of the past we can help to de-condition specific memories...once we have worked with as many memories as we can...then we could always do this for a general sense of the past too that's not generally the way we use this method....it's really meant to deal with specific memories...

I have a client (young man 21) who has terrible fear of death. He doesn't do anything that could be "dangerous" like going to a roller coaster last summer (something he has been able to do before). He ruminates about death and dying at night and does not sleep well. He is afraid of his own death and his loved ones. He says it freaks him out that you will be dead forever. No after life. He has difficulty listening to songs about death. The only person he knows that has died

was his grandfather and then my client was 7 years old. He says that is the time he started to think about death. I would like some tips on using the Rewind Technique for this problem. Another question: I finished level 1 and 2 in EMDR. I own theratapper that I often use when creating safe place and when relaxing my clients. What about using them (BLS) when doing Rewind? Any thoughts on that?

I think there is a point in everyone's life, or anyone who can think and imagine abstractly, where you become aware of your own mortality. I recall crying for hours at the age of three over the realisation that I was finite. It feels so counterintuitive that we, the centre of awareness, won't be here. I got over that when my sister who is a year older reminded me that I had to grow up first, a great example of a therapeutic reframe from a four year old! And being a grown up was so infinitely far away to me then that it was the equivalent to living forever anyway.

Fear of death, above and beyond the feeling we might get if we think we are just about to die or have been told by a doctor we will soon pass away...the kind of fear of death in a healthy and safe person...is really common. I wrote an article about how to overcome this kind of, what we might call unreasonable fear of death and almost 300 people have commented so it's a preoccupation or focus of rumination or for some people OBSESSION that is common.

As far as using Rewind is concerned you would need, I think, to ascertain whether he has memories of his grandfather dying that are particularly troublesome and still hurt to recall or whether he has an imagined scenario that he's traumatised himself with. If so, you could Rewind the fearful fantasies he has scared himself with if they are actually NARRATIVE memories. There's no guarantee of course that he WON'T experience an afterlife but we can't rely on that; all of us have I think at least got to be prepared for annihilation. The billions of years, well presumably eternal time, he wasn't here BEFORE he was born weren't too bad, but another idea I like to present to healthy clients who misuse their imaginations around death is of the way nature gives us compensations sometimes to make experiences easier than they would be.

So when it comes time, it feels right. When it comes time it FEELS right. Of course it doesn't feel right to a healthy 3 year old or a healthy 21 year old, it feels the most unnatural thing in the world, but during extreme life threat we may have a kind of strange calm or transcendent feeling. Someone told me she almost drowned and in that moment she was suffused by a sense of universal love, a feeling of unity, oneness and deep peace. She was resuscitated but strangely it was the happiest experience of her life, not that she wanted to die.

Dying at 90 or 103 once the body has been used up will feel right because it will be natural in that context. This is an idea he might not have considered carefully.

Death might not feel right now in the middle of health and vitality and life, but nature has its compensations. We need to surrender to some of the ebbs and flows and rhythms of life.

Research has shown that calmly reflecting on your own mortality makes people happier and more productive. So it's not that we should NEVER be aware we are finite but that when we do this we should reflect on it calmly.

According to the research carried out in 2011 and published in The Journal of Positive Psychology reflecting on death calmly helped people become happier because it enabled them to prioritise what they really want to do in life. Calm death awareness helps us live better, but also feel more grateful and we know from research that gratitude tracks alongside happiness.

Tell your client of the benefits of calm death reflection. Have him practice it with you calmly during hypnosis whilst also visualizing what he wants to do in LIFE. Have him do calm death reflecting every day at a set time for ten minutes. If thoughts of death come to mind at any other time he's to remind himself that he needs to save those thoughts up for the ten minute slot. In this way we are starting to ORGANIZE the rumination so he runs it and not the other way around.

So to summarize:

Ascertain whether there is a memory or fantasy narrative in need of Rewind.

Talk to him about nature's compensations. When something feels right it IS right in nature.

Talk to him about the research that tells us doing death reflection properly in a limited way enhances gratitude and motivation to truly live whilst we are here. And have him practice that whilst deeply relaxed.

Give him the task of reflecting in this way for ten minutes a day calmly and if thoughts try to intrude outside of his reflection time or meditation on death time he is to remind himself he needs to save those thoughts up and watch them calmly in his allotted time.

A worry is only a worry because of the feeling we have in CONJUNCTION with the imagining or thought but if we calm the feeling the imaging or through can remain, without the feeling, this is what you are teaching him to do.

And the last part of your question, if I understand it, do we need to do EMDR or eye movement desensitization reprocessing whilst doing Rewind? I would say not at all. EMDR isn't as complete or comprehensive a process as Rewind and you will often see rapid eye movement occurring in clients when you do Rewind with them because you are asking them to visualize. We don't need to artifactually induce rapid eye movement in our clients as part of Rewind.

I would like to ask about using Rewind for children? Any specialist tips on that?

It depends how old the child is. All we need to do is adapt our language, so instead of using words like relax I might use phrases like "feeling happy and brave.." or "feeling sleepy and happy..." Because young children are so naturally aligned to their imaginations, using this approach for traumatized or phobic children tends to be even easier, and we can adapt Rewind.

For example, I had a nine year old boy who had severe emetophobia (fear of vomiting) in his case OTHER people vomiting. He didn't want to go to school or to friend's houses and he had some traumatic memories of his sister having vomited.

I talked to him about his favorite action star and asked him how this action star would have dealt with the boy's sister being sick. He said that he would have been calm and brave. I then had him close his eyes and imagine becoming that action star then as the action star to go into his sitting room at home and drift into the screen at the end of the memory and go backwards in time being that action star helping his sister calmly in backwards time, then to drift out of that and watch himself, still as the action star, in fast forward being really cool and heroic in those times and so on.

I got him to experience internalizing the parts of the action star that were brave and calm and did plenty of positive rehearsal of future vomiting times. So I really incorporated his hero into the narrative of the technique. He went back to school and started seeing his friends again and positively wanted the chance to be brave and calm.

I sometimes talk to older clients about old style video recorders and obviously for younger clients that doesn't make sense, but we can talk about going backwards in time or seeing a film really fast and being separate from it. So simple language, adapt your language where appropriate, and incorporate elements from story books or movie characters the child identifies with and be creative with it because children ARE creative.

I'm working with a lady with a eating disorder and I'm wondering if the Rewind Technique could help (i.e. rewind the movie from the time it started to now). What do you think? Have you tried it for eating disorders or would you recommend something else?

Well the Rewind is really most effective for really strong trauma, the kind of memory that makes a person terrified. Many eating disorders work more like addictions. Just as when dealing with, say, smoking, I would externalize the pattern. How does the eating disorder convince you to follow its diktat? You know that kind of thing, removing it from her core identity. I also suggest you Google "molar memories" and watch Joe Griffin talk about that on video or read about it. Sometimes these kinds of compulsions seem to have a double rooted memory. A molar memory is one that has both a positive and negative emotional root and seems to produce bafflingly compulsive behaviours. Many fetishes and other compulsions may have originated from molar memories. Often the unpleasant memory is easily consciously recalled but not the pleasant one.

For example, I worked with a woman who would compulsively chew discarded rubber bands and smoke thrown-away cigarettes. She had enough money not to do this and was at a loss as to where the compulsion to do both could have come from.

I did an affect bridge with her by asking her to focus in on the feeling of wanting to pick up discarded cigarettes or rubber bands to chew. She accessed the feeling and I asked her to trace the feeling back to a memory, or at least to see if any memory came to mind. At first she told me no memory had come to mind. But after a few more seconds, she suddenly recalled a time at school when friends had thrown away sweets in the playground and she had greedily scooped them up to eat (her step mother who was very controlling never allowed her sweets or even gifts on her birthday.). The other children had laughed at her and she had felt terrible shame, and that shame seemed to be the root of the behaviour. But I asked her to recall the other emotional root to the memory, how had she felt BEFORE the other children had discovered her scooping up and devouring all those thrown away sweets.

She was surprised to recall the wonderful excitement and happiness she had felt and suddenly being able to have something for herself. So we see here the shame wasn't the only feeling associated with the genesis of this compulsion but also the excitement which was the part of the memory she hadn't thought of in a long time. I asked her to say aloud a few times that she was now a grown up and could buy what she needed for herself.

I suspect this was an example of a 'molar memory' – one that has both a positive and negative emotional root and seems to produce bafflingly compulsive behaviours. And sometimes we find this is the case in the genesis of eating disorders . So that might be worth exploring. But you could certainly try Rewind too to try and take out the emotional pull of the behaviour.

But, of course, when working with memories we need to ensure we are helping the client access memories they have always had – because in therapy we always need to remain aware of the very real risk of manufacturing memories especially if we are doing inner work with them.

So try Rewind. Work to remove the condition from her core identity in the way you talk about it to her. Think of the possibility of a molar memory as a driver for the compulsion, and follow up Joe Griffin's work on molar memories. Try to work out what needs the compulsion, the eating disorder, seem to meet and how she can meet those in legitimate and healthy ways."

How do you deal with memory/experience where, following the rewind, the memory or SUDS level is still quite high and has stayed high by the next session. Would you keep rewinding on the same memories until they're reduced or change tack and do something else?

. . .

SUDS (Subjective Units of Discomfort), so what we often do with the Rewind Technique is say "if you think about that memory now, if 10 is the most terrified as it may have been at the time, and 1 is the most relaxed? What does it feel when you think about it now, not what it was at the time, but what is it now when you think about it?" And someone might say well it's a 7 or 8, some people say 10, some people say more than 10! And then after you've done the Rewind you ask "what is it now?" and it might be a 2 or a 3.

Usually after Rewind, arousal around the memory you have worked on goes down considerably when, perhaps especially when, dealing with extreme trauma.

So it might go from say a 10 out of 10 to a 3/10 or even to a level so low the person can no longer put a number on it. Occasionally it might only go down a few points. We can do two things here. We can suggest it will continue to go down over the next few days.

We are looking, of course, to turn the memory from an experiential one which feels more like a reliving of the initial experience rather than a recalling of it - otherwise known as a flashback - into a narrative memory which is no longer played out in the Amygdala (fight or flight part of the brain). So typically, people after Rewind will report that the memory no longer feels threatening, they feel calm when they think about it now or that it seems far away. Because of this change nightmares stop and so do flashbacks because the person's brain is no longer trying desperately to contextualise what happened to them because you have helped them do that for them.

If it has only gone down a bit then certainly do more Rewind. Eventually it's as though the person becomes bored with the memory which is a much better outcome than being terrified of it. If Rewind doesn't seem to be working then it may be because you haven't spent enough time helping them relax deeply and more focus needs to be done on that part of the process. But if something isn't working then it's always worth looking to do something else because we need to respond flexibly to our clients.

Sometimes, very occasionally though, something quite strange happens. I recall doing Rewind as a demonstration for a woman who had a phobia of going down escalators on the London underground or subway as it's called in the USA. After Rewind, she said the SUDS (Subjective Units of Discomfort) hadn't gone down much at all. So, you know as a demonstration it wasn't that dramatic. But a few months later the same woman came back on another workshop I was running and reminded me of the work we'd done and said that she had decided to go down into the London Underground, and to her amazement had felt not the slightest flicker of anxiety or fear when going down the deep escalators. So SUDS can sometimes be misleading and it may be that the person's mind needs to assimilate the changes over the slightly longer term.

Are there any circumstances where this technique (reframing and Rewind) is counterproductive?

All therapy, in fact all psychological growth, tracks alongside being able to see flexibly and from multiple or wider perspectives. Depressive perspectives for example tend to be stereotypical and therefore rigid.

So depressive perception tends toward the all or nothing. Completely this or completely that, black or white. Negatives are seen as sustainable and perhaps permanent, positives are seen as fragile and unlikely to last and on top of that positive opportunities to meet emotional needs may even be seen as negatives. So the way reality is perceived is narrowed thanks to the pervasiveness of the emotions and learning which drive depressive thought.

Certainly we need to help people reframe or widen the frame of the way they see reality. We can do this both by helping change the emotion so it feels more natural to think differently as when we use Rewind to de-traumatise or take the fear from a phobia and then find that the client inevitably views the situation of former phobic stimulus differently because the feelings have changed.

But we can also help our clients examine their assumptions and widen their perspectives by directly working on the cognitive level of the person. We work on the emotional, cognitive and behavioural elements.

But the way we reframe needs to be respectful and effective. We don't just suggest people see something differently because to do so is tantamount to saying: "You are wrong for thinking this!" If someone says to me: "I believe in God or I don't believe in God" I am not going to build or maintain rapport with them by simply telling them they are mistaken in their belief, and it's the same with limiting beliefs. If someone tells me they are a bad person it can be terribly rapport breaking to tell them they are wrong about that. But to show them their picture may be incomplete is another matter. Real reframing is about showing, not telling, and we can do this through metaphor, humour, Socratic questioning and so forth. But as with everything, timing is vital.

If someone has just had a bereavement or needs understanding and sympathy first then trying to help them see a situation differently too prematurely may at best fall on deaf ears or at worst break any sense of being understood. When someone is off loading they may just need to be listened to for a while.

Eventually they may need to see things more flexibly or less pervasively. So it's not that we wouldn't use reframing but we might have to wait to use it. So too early attempts at reframing might be counterproductive.

As to whether using the Rewind technique would ever be counterproductive and therefore contraindicated I'd say that really it's a method to treat strong Post Traumatic Stress Disorder and phobias so it wouldn't be necessarily counter productive to use it for other emotional conditions but it might be unnecessary.

I am curious to know whether you have treated many war veterans and if the Rewind Technique has been helpful to all or the majority of them. There has recently been a lot of publicity about the experience of war and related PTSD and tragically the suicide of many people who have lived in torment and found that to be the only answer. I feel that I should be doing more to help in this area. Your thoughts and recommendations would be much appreciated.

I have only treated maybe a dozen or so over the years and a couple of civilians who had been caught up in war zones, including one who had been kidnapped and believed during that time he faced imminent execution. I have found war veterans extremely easy to treat using rewind. One man I treated in the 1990's had PTSD relating to an incident which had occurred in the 1940's during World War 2! And I know a practitioner in the States used Rewind to help a man who was still having flashbacks and nightmares relating to The Vietnam war. It is a tragedy and a travesty that so many war vets remain untreated but usually the first line of treatment is drug treatment or many remain untreated or may self medicate with alcohol or drugs. You could certainly advertise that you are happy to work with traumatised war vets.

Is it possible to use this technique on yourself? Can I create a recording? Looking forward to your thoughts.

Yes indeed it is possible to use it on yourself as I used it on myself many years ago to overcome a lifelong fear of public speaking and now, for better or for worse for those who listen to me :) I find I just CAN'T feel nervous anymore when public speaking. Before using REWIND make sure it really is a fear you want rid of because you might not be able to get it back! :) I used it on myself by just going through the process because I know it so well but if you are new to it then you could record yourself and listen to the recording later....that would be a great way of doing it.

Can the Rewind Technique help someone with grief, someone who's lost a loved one just eight weeks ago and how many sessions would it take?

. . .

Right, okay. Well, with grief, we can't assume that post-traumatic stress disorder is there with grief. The way to ascertain that, I think, is the person able to think about the person's life or is it just the way they died that comes to mind?

So, you might have a client that comes along and all they can think about is images and images of their loved one lying in hospital with lots of tubes going into them. Or they may have even found their loved one dead in the house or whatever and that's what comes to mind. And in a sense, that's blocking the grieving process because if they have nightmares about that constantly and flashbacks and they keep getting reminded of it, keep having these spontaneous hypnotic regressions back to that particular time - which is what a flashback is, really, a sort of spontaneous hypnotic regression - then you would need to work on that before they can grieve. So PTSD isn't necessarily a part of the grieving process, but it can block the beginnings of the grieving process. You might have to do that, but you can't assume that it's there.

Can they think about the person's life? When they think about them, they might really, really miss them and that isn't the same as being traumatized in that way. It's a natural shock when someone dies, because you're used to having them be there. But it's very different from a young person having a catastrophic death that was totally unexpected to a very old person who you knew it was coming for a long time. It can still be heartbreaking for the person grieving that person, but it's not necessarily the same as a sudden shock death in which perhaps they witnessed something as well. So, you wouldn't necessarily, as par of the course, use Rewind with all grieving clients, but you'd have to ascertain that.

And then, once you do that, once you treat the memory, then the person is freed up to appreciate the person's life, not just focus on the way that they died. A metaphor I often use is that if you have a favorite book, then you've always got that book and you can reread chapters again and everything, but you don't just have to focus on the full stop, the way the book ended, the full stop. You can enjoy the rest of the book now and forget about the full stop once we've got the trauma out of the way. But the trauma isn't necessarily there, that's the thing to remember.

Would Rewind be suitable for someone who has come with a fear of flying but all his anxiety seems to stem from enclosed spaces? He never liked going in the back of 2 door cars as a child and now can't do it at all.

Many frightened flyers have a control issue and say they would be okay if they could get off anytime they wanted to. It's a mistake I think to assume that flying phobics all fear the plane crashing or even being up high. I would most definitely rewind past memories of having been terrified during flights but I would also hypnotically discuss the idea that inwardly we all have the space of the universe in our minds. Someone can be sitting in a plane and watching a movie or reading a novel and be more psychologically attuned to the places and people of that movie or novel than they are to the reality of the plane around them. For a while we humans can forget to remember our present reality and take journeys inwardly to any place or time. When your client dreams at night he has all the space in the universe, he can be anywhere and for a while he forgets to remember the bed he's in or the room he is sleeping in. This capacity human beings have of transcending the present time and space is what has enabled us to rise out of the swamps and create and build and enhance life in many ways.

If I take a long flight I don't want to be on that flight all that time. I want to focus my mind beyond the boredom of the flight to other times and realities and that's when time flies.

So I talk a lot to clients about "time flying". If I have psychologically removed myself from the flight by reading a book or watching a film then time seems to fly. So you can make hypnotic suggestions for this - that we all have infinite space within us wherever we happen to be physically, but I would do this after you have rewound any terrifying memories he might have.

THIRTEEN

THE NEXT STEP

In this book we have touched upon the many faces of trauma – and the unifying concepts that can help you treat it comfortably and effectively, no matter what caused it or how severe its effects.

But it doesn't end here. Join me on our Rewind Technique course to learn in greater detail how you can apply this detraumatizing technique in your own practice. You'll get access to our online training platform Uncommon U, comprehensive course notes, demonstration videos with real clients and more. You'll also be able to ask any questions you may have, both through the dedicated forums and the live Q&A sessions.

I hope to see you there!

P.S. I publish a free weekly therapy tips newsletter containing articles like those in this book. You can sign up here.

NOTES

Introduction

1. Dodge, C. P., & Raundalen, M. (1991). *Reaching children in war: Sudan, Uganda, and Mozambique*. Bergen, Norway: Sigma Forlag.

1. Popular treatment models for PTSD

1. Murphy, M. (2007). Testing treatment for trauma. *Human Givens*, 14(4), 37–42.

2. Is your client traumatized?

1. Wilson, J. P., & Keane, T. M. (1997). *Assessing psychological trauma and PTSD*. New York: The Guilford Press.
2. Wilson & Keane, *Assessing psychological trauma and PTSD*.
3. Spiegel, D., Detrick, D., & Frischholz, E. J. (1982). Hypnotizability and psychopathology. *American Journal of Psychiatry*, 139, 431–437.
4. Wilson & Keane, *Assessing psychological trauma and PTSD*.
5. Van der Kolk et al., B. A., McFarlane, A. C., & Weisaeth, L. (Eds.) (1996). *Traumatic stress*. New York: The Guilford Press.

5. Why there's no need to relive the trauma all over again

1. Rose, S., Bisson, J., Churchill, R., & Wessely, S. (2002). Psychological debriefing for preventing post traumatic stress disorder (PTSD). *Cochrane Database Syst Rev*, 2002;(2):CD000560.
2. Griffin, J., & Tyrrell, I. (2003). *Human Givens: A new approach to emotional health and clear thinking* (p. 282). East Sussex: HG Publishing.
3. Wilson & Keane, *Assessing psychological trauma and PTSD*.
4. Shapiro, F., & Forrest, M. S. (1997). *EMDR: the breakthrough therapy for overcoming anxiety, stress, and trauma*. New York: Basic Books.
5. The Human Givens Institute (n. d.). *The 'rewind' technique*. Retrieved from http://www.hgi.org.uk/archive/rewind-technique.htm

6. Elliott, R. (n. d.). *Phobias – Strange but simple, terrible but treatable.* Retrieved from http://www.uncommon-knowledge.co.uk/phobias.html

6. Why I never have my clients relive their traumatic experiences

1. Rose et al., Psychological debriefing for preventing post traumatic stress disorder (PTSD).
2. *See* Ignaz Semmelweis (n.d.). In *Wikipedia.* Retrieved from https://en.wikipedia.org/wiki/Ignaz_Semmelweis [Semmelweis was a pioneer of antiseptic procedure.]

7. Why PTSD and phobias are a case of bad hypnosis

1. Yard, S. S., DuHamel, K. N., Galynker, I. I. (2008). Hypnotizability as a potential risk factor for posttraumatic stress: A review of quantitative studies. *International Journal of Clinical and Experimental Hypnosis,* 56(3), 334–56.

8. Is trauma locking your client in depression?

1. *See* Bergland, C. (2013). *Cortisol: Why "The Stress Hormone" Is Public Enemy No. 1.* Retrieved from https://www.psychologytoday.-com/blog/the-athletes-way/201301/cortisol-why-the-stress-hormone-is-public-enemy-no-1
2. See *How depression works – the cycle of depression* (n.d.). Retrieved from http://www.clinical-depression.co.uk/cycle-of-depression-diagram/ [The 'Cycle of Depression' shows how this works.]
3. These needs were identified by Human Givens psychologists Joe Griffin and Ivan Tyrrell (my father).

10. Encouraging post-traumatic growth in your client

1. Taleb, N. N. (2012). *Antifragile: Things That Gain from Disorder.* London: Penguin. [This is a wonderful book.]
2. Wolff's Law (n.d.). In *Wikipedia.* Retrieved on September 25, 2015, from https://en.wikipedia.org/wiki/Wolff%27s_law

ABOUT MARK TYRRELL

PTSD: Horror in the Mind was written by Mark Tyrrell of Uncommon Knowledge.

Mark has been working as a therapist and trainer since 1995. He has given lectures to thousands of health professionals on self esteem, detraumatization, and workplace bullying.

Since co-founding Uncommon Knowledge with Roger Elliott, Mark has run their Diploma in Solution-Focused Psychotherapy and Hypnotherapy for ten years, authored *New Ways of Seeing*, co-authored *The Giant Within*, and created over 500 hours of self help videos.

Mark also writes a blog at Uncommon Practitioners and delivers online training in therapy skills. You can subscribe to his weekly email newsletter on therapy tips here.

Each year, more than 100,000 people subscribe to Mark's

online courses, and over 10 million visit Uncommon Knowledge's psychology and therapy websites.

When he has a spare moment, Mark enjoys playing tennis and training in obscure martial arts.

- facebook.com/uncommonknowledge
- twitter.com/unktweets
- instagram.com/marktyrrellunk
- linkedin.com/in/mark-tyrrell
- amazon.com/Mark-Tyrrell/e/B001H9PBL6
- bookbub.com/profile/mark-tyrrell

ALSO BY MARK TYRRELL

New Ways of Seeing: The Art of Therapeutic Reframing: How to use your words to release your clients from limiting beliefs, including examples from 81 real cases.

Uncommon Practitioners Series

The Dark Side of The Human Needs: Help Clients Answer the Question 'Why Do I Do That?' and Stop Self Sabotage

Printed in Dunstable, United Kingdom

76881646R00061